J 550.78 WOO

Wood, Robert W., 1933-

39 easy geology
  experiments /

CENTRAL-J

21 x 6/99 LT 3/99
25 x 12/00 LT 10/00
36 x 9/04 LT 4/04

D1441895

Science for Kids
39 EASY
GEOLOGY EXPERIMENTS

Science for Kids
39 EASY
GEOLOGY EXPERIMENTS

Robert W. Wood
Illustrations by Steve Hoeft

TAB BOOKS
Blue Ridge Summit, PA

FIRST EDITION
FIRST PRINTING

© 1991 by **TAB Books**.
TAB Books is a division of McGraw-Hill, Inc.

Printed in the United States of America. All rights reserved. The publisher takes no responsibility for the use of any of the materials or methods described in this book, nor for the products thereof.

Library of Congress Cataloging-in-Publication Data

Wood, Robert W., 1933-
   Science for kids : 39 easy geology experiments / by Robert W. Wood.
     p. cm.
   Includes index.
   Summary: Experiments to introduce the student to geology include testing aluminum for corrosion, texting granite for hardness, growing crystals, and making concrete.
   ISBN 0-8306-6598-6 (h)   ISBN 0-8306-3598-X (p)
   1. Geology—Experiments—Juvenile literature. [1. Geology—Experiments. 2. Experiments.] I. Title.
QE29.W66 1991   91-7418
507.8—dc20   CIP
                                     AC

TAB Books offers software for sale. For information and a catalog, please contact TAB Software Department, Blue Ridge Summit, PA 17294-0850.

Acquisitions Editor: Kimberly Tabor
Book Editor: Nina Barr
Production: Katherine G. Brown
Book Design: Jaclyn J. Boone
Cover photography courtesy of Susan Riley, Harrisonburg, VA.

Contents

Introduction

The Science For Kids series consists of eight books introducing astronomy, chemistry, meteorology, geology, engineering, plant biology, animal biology, and geography.

Science is a subject that becomes instantly exciting with even the simplest discoveries. On any day, and at any time, we can see these mysteries unfold around us.

The series was written to open the door and to invite the curious to enter—to explore, to think, and to wonder. To realize that anyone, absolutely anyone at all, can experiment and learn. To discover that the only thing you really need to study science is an inquiring mind. The rest of the material is all around you, there for anyone to see. You have only to look.

This book, *39 Easy Geology Experiments,* will introduce you to the fascinating world of geology. Scientists have found evidence that fixes the age of the earth at about four and a half billion years. In that time, lava has flowed from pockets of molten rock several miles underground. Wide rivers of ice have moved down mountainsides and through valleys, breaking off blocks of rock and prying others out of the ground. Seas have moved across sinking continents, leaving layers of sand and mud that later turned into land. This land was worn by rain and wind. Streams made gullies that grew into ravines and canyons, and land heaved and crumpled, forming ranges of mountains. In doing this, the earth has written its entire history in the rocks and rock formations. Our earth is still constantly changing.

Experiments 1 and 2 demonstrate how rain wears at the soil and how the earth shifts and moves under pressure to create mountains and valleys. This motion causes some land masses to sink and allows water to flow in, creating bodies of water we know as seas and lakes.

Geology is the science that studies these changes while they are happening as well as the result of those changes. It also includes the study of the fossils of living things and their surroundings. Fossils help geologists to determine the age of rock formations, because each division of the earth's history had plants and animals that lived at no other time.

Most of us often overlook the important contributions geologists make. But when we look around, we see we rely upon geology every day. Plaster that covers the walls in our buildings is made in part from two rocks, gypsum and limestone. Experiment 18 explains what gypsum is, and Experiment 25 shows how limestone is used for specific building projects.

The concrete in the foundations of buildings contains cement made from limestone and shale. Deposits of iron, copper, and clay discovered by geologists provide the steel for the structures, copper for the pipes, and the clay for the plumbing fixtures and tile found in our schools. Geologists found oil deposits which bring us materials for composition shingles, oil and gasoline for the trucks that haul the materials for the buildings, and even the asphalt for roads used by the trucks.

It is easy to see how important geology is to oil and mining companies, but geologists also perform state and national geological surveys, teach at universities, and are even consultants to city water departments. Geology is, indeed, an important science that affects our daily lives.

In about 1795, a former doctor and farmer, James Hutton of Scotland, published a book declaring that streams and rivers wore deep gorges, and that sandstone was nothing more than hardened beds of sand, and that ancient rocks, such as basalt, were like lava from volcanoes. He said that the earth is still changing, as it has in the past, forming new rocks and wearing away the old.

In 1830, Charles Lyell published a book called Principles of Geology where he agreed with Hutton and further added that while waves destroy rocky seashores, they build up beaches and sandbars. Both proved that the earth is changing now, and that in order to learn what happened in the past, we must study what is happening now.

The study of geology can be thought of as an adventure, but a safe adventure. Don't go on field trips alone. Tell someone where you're going and when you'll be back. Geology is a science of discovery and is best when shared with someone. But remember, always be safe.

Be sure to read the Symbols Used in This Book section that follows before you begin any experiments. It warns you of all the safety precautions you should consider before you begin a project and whether or not you should have a teacher, parent, or other adult to help you.

Completely read through a project before you begin to be sure you understand the experiment and you have all of the materials you'll need. Each experiment has a materials list and easy, step-by-step instruction with illustrations to help you.

Although you will want to pick a project that interests you, you might want to do some of the projects in order. It isn't necessary, but some of the principles you learn in the first few experiments will provide you with some basic understanding of geology and help you do later experiments.

Symbols Used in This Book

All of the experiments in this book can be done safely, but young children should be instructed to respect the hazards associated with careless use. The following symbols are used throughout the book for you to use as a guide to what children might be able to do independently, and what they *should not do* without adult supervision. Keep in mind that some children might not be mature enough to do any of the experiments without adult help, and that these symbols should be used as a guide only and do not replace good judgment of parents or teachers.

Materials or tools used in this experiment could be dangerous in young hands. Adult supervision is recommended. Children should be instructed on the care and handling of sharp tools or combustible or toxic materials and how to protect surfaces.

Protective safety goggles should be worn to protect against shattering glass or other hazards that could damage the eyes.

The use of the stove, boiling water, or other hot materials are used in this project and adult supervision is required. Keep other small children away from boiling water and burners.

1

Soil Erosion

Materials
a small area of bare
soil
an equal area of soil
with grass
water hose with
adjustable nozzle

Adjust the nozzle of the water hose to a spray similar to rainfall, and spray the bare soil a few minutes. Soon gullies will form, and the soil will begin to wash away. Now spray the grassy area for about the same period of time. You will see a little of the soil washing away. The blades of grass soften the fall of water, and the roots help hold the soil together. You also can make furrows along the contours of the bare ground to prevent the soil from washing away and to conserve water for plants.

Erosion is the wearing away of the earth. It is mostly caused by wind and water. Large, deep-rooted trees have been slowly buried and killed by wind-blown sand, and farms have been abandoned after the fertile soil was washed away by wind or rain.

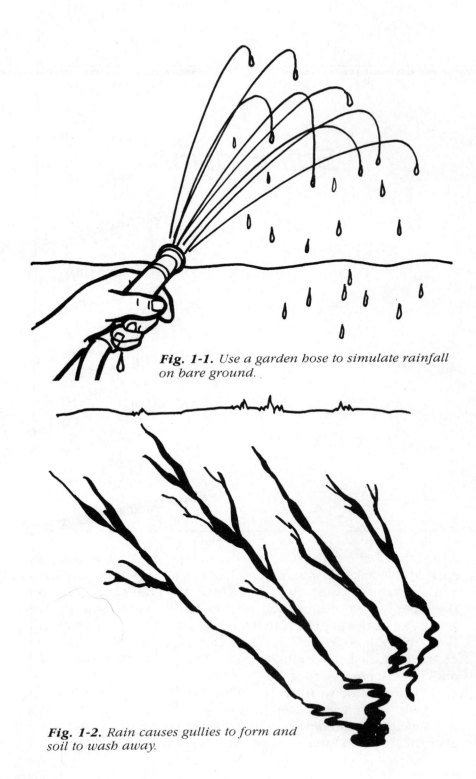

Fig. 1-1. *Use a garden hose to simulate rainfall on bare ground.*

Fig. 1-2. *Rain causes gullies to form and soil to wash away.*

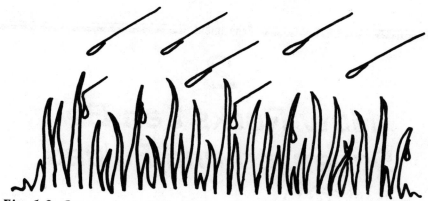

Fig. 1-3. *Grass softens the force of rain and helps hold the soil together.*

2
How Rocks Can Be Squeezed and Folded

Materials

modeling clay
(3 different colors)

tablespoon

Roll each color clay into strips and build up layers of different colors. Push the layers from the ends until they start to fold. The shallow, up and down folds are called *upright anticlines* and *synclines*. Continue pushing from the ends until a fold begins to roll over. This fold is called an *overfold*. If you keep pushing and the layers begin to tear, it will become a faulted fold or a thrust-faulted fold. Now use the spoon to carve formations in the clay such as mountains and valleys. You will see how the different layers of rock make the various patterns often seen where highways are cut through mountains.

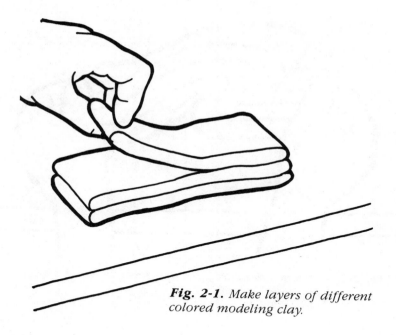

Fig. 2-1. *Make layers of different colored modeling clay.*

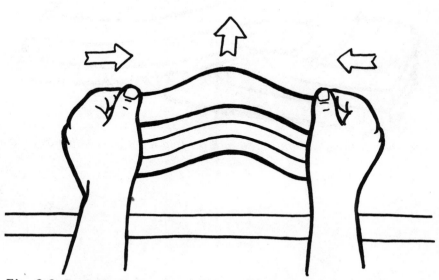

Fig. 2-2. *Push the layers together from the ends to make the folds called anticlines and synclines.*

Fig. 2-3. *Continued pressure from the ends will cause an overfold.*

Fig. 2-4. *If pressure continues until the fold tears, it is called a faulted fold.*

Fig. 2-5. Sections cut from the clay will show patterns similar to those found in layers of rock.

3
Why Rocks Break Apart

Materials

Small glass bottle with screw on lid

Paper towels

refrigerator

water

Fill the bottle completely full of water and screw the lid on tightly. Wrap a couple of paper towels around the bottle and place the bottle in the freezing compartment of a refrigerator over night. Now carefully unfold the paper towels and examine the bottle. It will be broken in several pieces. When the water froze, it expanded and broke the bottle. After you have finished, throw the towels and broken glass in the trash.

Water often seeps into the cracks in a rock. If the water freezes, it will expand with a tremendous force and cause the cracks to grow bigger and longer. This expansion force can break rocks into smaller pieces.

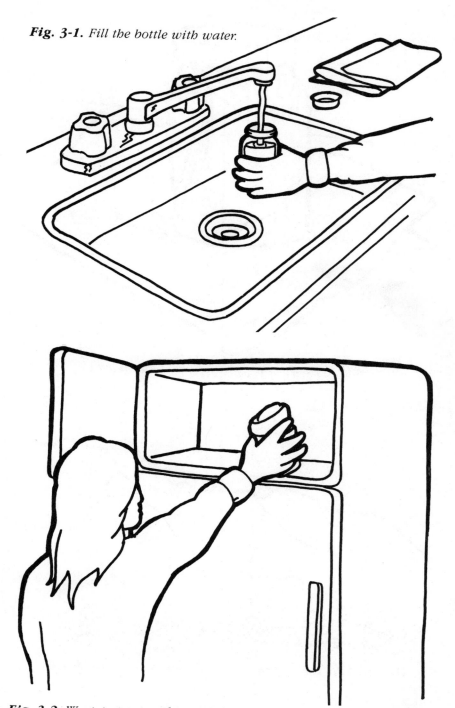

Fig. 3-1. Fill the bottle with water.

Fig. 3-2. Wrap paper towels around the bottle and place it in the freezer.

Fig. 3-3. *When the water froze it expanded.*

Fig. 3-4. *Cracks in rocks often contain moisture. If it freezes, it can split the rocks.*

Sun shining on a rock will cause the surface of the rock to get hotter than the inner part of the rock. This heat makes the outer part of the rock expand more than the inside part. This expansion can cause the rock to crack. At night, the outer part of the rock cools faster than the inner part. This cooling causes the outer part to contract more than the inside, and more cracks can form. You might have seen places where large sheets of rock have split away and tumble down the side of a hill.

4
Materials in Soil

Materials

magnifying glass
piece of white paper
small amount of
dry soil

Spread a little soil on the paper and examine it with the magnifying glass. Look for small pieces of sand, humus, and clay. The sand will be in the form of tiny grains of glasslike particles that can have sharp or rounded corners. *Humus* is a brown or black substance that forms from the partial decay of plant or animal matter. It is the organic part of the soil. Clay is usually lighter than the color of humus. It might be too fine for you to see with a magnifying glass.

Soil is made up of sand or clay, or both, mixed with humus. Often the top layer of soil, called the *topsoil*, contains a lot of humus. The layer of soil just below the topsoil is called the *subsoil*. It usually contains little or no humus.

Fig. 4-1. *Spread a little soil on a white paper.*

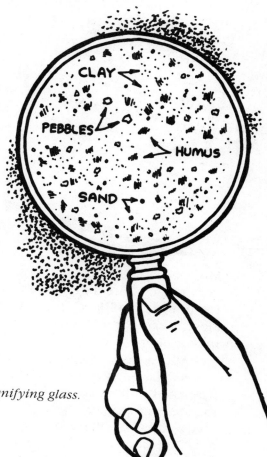

CLAY

PEBBLES

HUMUS

SAND

Fig. 4-2. *Examine the soil with a magnifying glass.*

5

How Plants Break Up Rocks

Materials

cardboard box
(lid from shoe box)
plaster of paris
paper towels
lima bean seeds
water

Mix the plaster of paris with water until you have a creamy mixture. Pour this mixture into the box. Now lay a few lima bean seeds on top of the wet plaster. Spread them around so that they're not too close. Next, cover the seeds with layers of wet paper towels. Wet the towels occasionally to keep them moist for about a week.

After a week, check the growth of the beans and the condition of the plaster. Remove a couple of the seeds and notice what happened to the plaster. Wait a couple of more days and examine the seeds and plaster again. Continue to watch the growth of the seeds, and you will see the roots of the sprouts dig into the plaster to get minerals. The plaster is a form of rock. The roots, searching for food, help break up rocks.

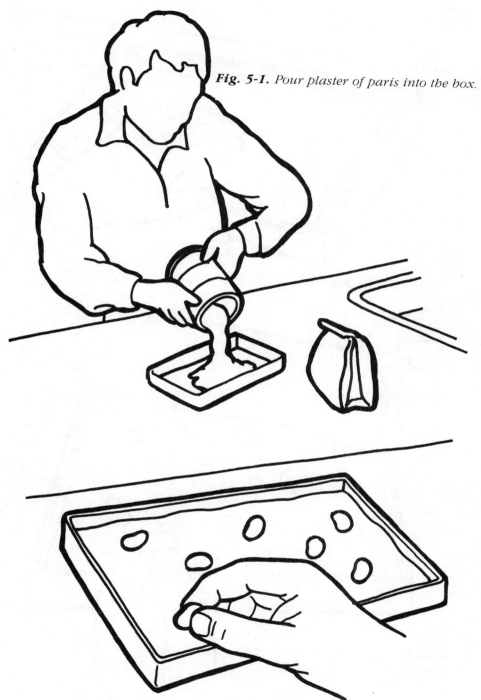

Fig. 5-1. *Pour plaster of paris into the box.*

Fig. 5-2. *Place lima beans on top of the wet plaster.*

Fig. 5-3. *Cover the beans with wet paper towels.*

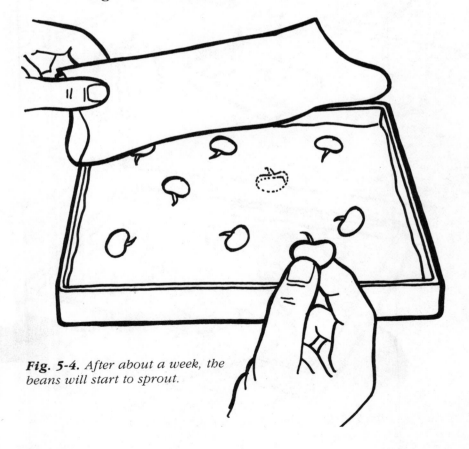

Fig. 5-4. *After about a week, the beans will start to sprout.*

Fig. 5-5. *The roots grow into the plaster and are strong enough to break it.*

6
How Water Separates Materials

Materials

soil
clear, glass jar
water
spoon

Fill the jar about one-third full of soil. Fill the jar the rest of the way up with water. Stir the water vigorously and let it stand a few days.

After the water has settled completely, and if the soil is rich, you will find the soil has been separated into layers. The top of the soil might have a thin layer of black carbon from the humus. The next layer down will contain fine mud, followed by grit and then small gravel at the bottom. Similar layers often can be found in sandstone.

Fig. 6-1. *Fill the jar part way with soil.*

Fig. 6-2. *Fill the rest of the jar with water and stir vigorously.*

Fig. 6-3. *When settling, the water separates the soil into layers.*

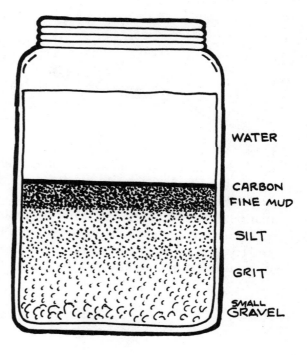

WATER

CARBON
FINE MUD

SILT

GRIT

SMALL
GRAVEL

7

Geology in Your Neighborhood

Materials

magnifying glass
notebook
pencil

Look for older public buildings in your neighborhood: schools, libraries, banks, or churches. Some might be made from local stone, but often polished, imported granite is used in banks and office buildings. Parks sometimes have statues made from fine marble. You also might find other decorative stones such as granite and limestone. Make a list of the different types of stone you find and try to learn where they came from. You might also want to note if any weathering has affected the stone and what caused the wear.

Fig. 7-1. *Statues and old buildings often are made from rocks such as marble and granite.*

Fig. 7-2. *Use a magnifying glass to examine the stones.*

Fig. 7-3. *A list will help you keep track of the different types of stones you find.*

8
Testing Water for Minerals

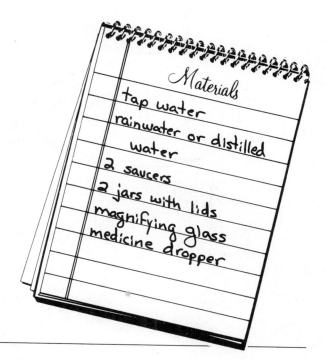

Materials

tap water
rainwater or distilled
water
2 saucers
2 jars with lids
magnifying glass
medicine dropper

Fill one jar with tap water and the other jar with rainwater. Now place several drops of tap water on one saucer and about the same amount of rainwater in the other saucer. Set both saucers aside until the water evaporates. Now use the magnifying glass to examine the rings left by the water. You will see that the tap water contained more minerals than the rainwater.

When water falls as rain, it contains no dissolved solid matter. Some of it runs off and finds its way into streams and rivers and eventually makes its way into lakes and oceans. The ground soaks up some of the water. Layers of clay or sand and the cracks in rocks store large amounts of water. Some of this water might have been locked under the ground for thousands of years. It could have

Fig. 8-1. *Place drops of different types of water on saucers.*

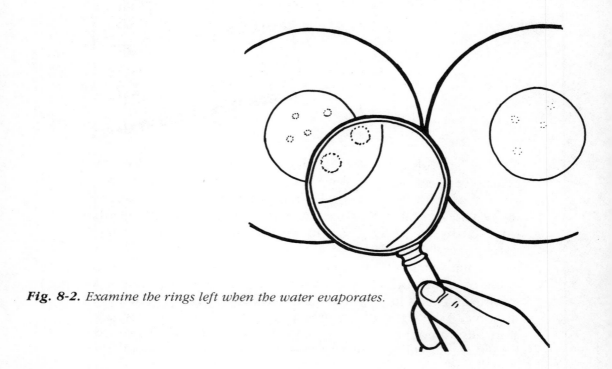

Fig. 8-2. *Examine the rings left when the water evaporates.*

Fig. 8-3. *Water makes a cycle between the oceans, clouds, rain, and then back to the oceans again.*

fallen as rain before the time of humans. Our water is continually making a cycle between the oceans, clouds, rain, streams, rivers, and lakes then back to the oceans again. It only changes its form and moves from place to place.

Because water dissolves many substances, a large number of these substances usually are present in natural water. The most common impurities are compounds of the chemicals: sodium, calcium, magnesium, and iron. Fortunately, these chemicals are not harmful to humans in small quantities.

9

Testing Water for Hardness

Materials

tap water
rainwater or distilled
   water
2 jars with lids
medicine dropper
liquid detergent
pencil and paper
spoon

Fill one jar about two-thirds full of tap water and pour an equal amount of rainwater into the other jar. Use the medicine dropper and add 2 drops of detergent to the tap water. Screw the lid on tight and shake the jar. If the detergent doesn't lather, add 2 more drops of detergent and shake the jar again. Continue to add detergent until it lathers. Now count the number of drops the water needed to produce a lather.

Repeat the same test with the rainwater and compare the number of drops of detergent used in each jar.

The water that required the most detergent is called *hard water*. This water should have been the tap water. Water that requires little soap to lather is called *soft water*.

Fig. 9-1. *Fill jars with equal amounts of tap water and rain water.*

Fig. 9-2. *Add two drops of detergent to the tap water.*

Fig. 9-3. Shake the jar to make a lather.

Fig. 9-4. Compare the number of drops of detergent required to make both types of water lather.

Fig. 9-5. *Washing soda helps hard water produce a lather.*

Calcium salts in the tap water keep the soap from lathering. If you add washing soda (sodium carbonate) to the tap water, the carbonate part of the soda mixes with the calcium in the water, making calcium carbonate. Now the calcium cannot react with the soap, and the soap can lather.

10
The Salty Ocean

Materials

cup
glass
teaspoon
tablespoon
1 teaspoon of table salt
10 tablespoons of water

Pour 1 teaspoon of salt into the cup and add 10 tablespoons of water. Stir the mixture thoroughly. Wet your finger in the water and taste the solution. This solution is about the same mixture as sea water. Ocean water contains about 3.5 percent salts; mostly, sodium chloride (table salt), potassium, and calcium salts along with magnesium salts. Every stream and river that flows into the ocean carries some amount of salt dissolved in it. It has been estimated that one-fourth of the material that the Mississippi River alone deposits in the sea is dissolved minerals. Small plants and animals, called *plankton*, use some of the salts. Chemical action of the sea water and sediment on the ocean floor also removes some of the salt, but very little of the sodium chloride is taken from the water.

Fig. 10-1. *Pour a teaspoon of salt into the cup.*

Fig. 10-2. *Add ten tablespoons of water.*

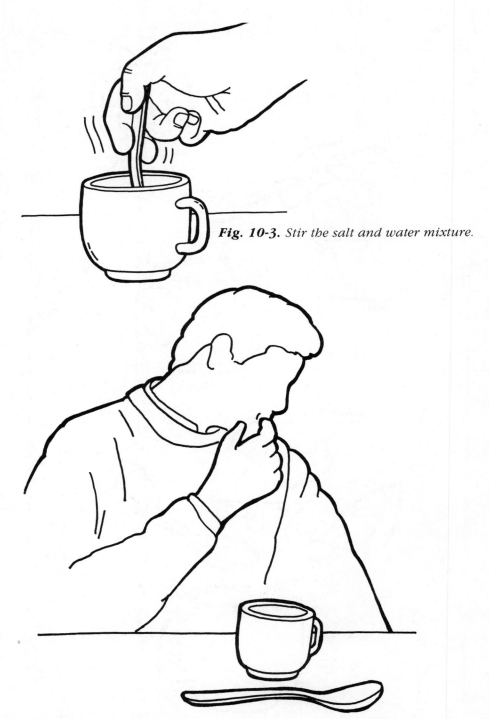

Fig. 10-3. *Stir the salt and water mixture.*

Fig. 10-4. *Taste the solution. It is about the same mixture as sea water.*

11
Looking at Salt

Materials

table salt
magnifying glass
piece of paper

Sprinkle a few grains of salt on the paper and examine them with the magnifying glass. You will see tiny cubelike crystals. The crystals are not transparent because of impurities. These crystals will not absorb water easily. Sometimes, however, tiny amounts of other minerals become mixed with the salt and they absorb moisture from the air. For this reason, on humid days, salt in a salt shaker becomes moist and lumpy.

Fig. 11-1. *Sprinkle a few grains of salt on a paper.*

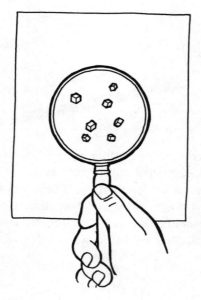

Fig. 11-2. *Examine the crystals with a magnifying glass.*

12
How Salt Crystals Form

Materials

3 tablespoons of soil
2 tablespoons of table salt
½ cup of water
saucer
glass
tablespoon
magnifying glass

Spread about 3 tablespoons of soil out in the saucer. Fill the glass about half full of water and add 2 tablespoons of salt. Stir the water several minutes to dissolve most of the salt. Let the water settle and then pour some of the clear salt water over the soil. Set the saucer in a warm place until the water evaporates and the mud is dry. Now examine the soil. At first, it might look like the tops of the small rocks were dusted with frost, but under the magnifying glass, you will see that they are topped by large crystals of salt called *rock salt*. More crystals will cover the rest of the soil. Rock salt is formed when minerals are dissolved in water. The salt water is drawn up through small openings in the soil and rocks by capillary action.

Fig. 12-1. *Place a little soil in a saucer and spread it out.*

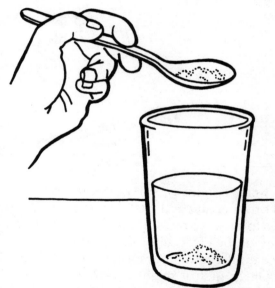

Fig. 12-2. *Add two tablespoons of salt to a half glass of water.*

The water then evaporates into the air leaving the salt behind. As the water evaporates, the molecules in the salt start to cling together and grow into larger crystals. The slower the evaporation, the larger the crystals.

Rock salt is made up of the mineral halite. It forms after long periods of evaporation of sea and lake water in an arid climate. Salt beds in such humid areas as New York, Ohio, and Michigan mean that the climate of those areas has changed since the beds were deposited.

Fig. 12-3. *Stir the water until most of the salt dissolves.*

Fig. 12-4. *Wet the soil with the salt water.*

Fig. 12-5. *Allow the mud to dry.*

Fig. 12-6. *Examine the soil for salt crystals.*

13
The Differences Between Rocks and Minerals

Materials

Salt crystal
quartz crystal
piece of granite
magnifying glass

Examine the salt crystal under the magnifying glass, and then examine the quartz crystal. Now look at the piece of granite. Compare the differences you see. The salt and quartz are minerals. The piece of granite is a rock. Minerals are the building blocks that make up rock. Some minerals are made from only one element, while others might consist of a complicated mixture of elements. Their individual make-up, however, is always the same. Table salt always has one atom of sodium for each atom of chlorine. Quartz is always made up of two-thirds oxygen and one-third silicon. Rocks, however, are almost always made up of a mixture of minerals.

Because rocks are formed in different ways than minerals, their mixtures can vary. The piece of granite probably consists of about 75 percent feldspar, about 20 percent quartz, and about 5 percent mica. Unlike minerals, the proportions do vary, and rocks can consist also of small amounts of other minerals.

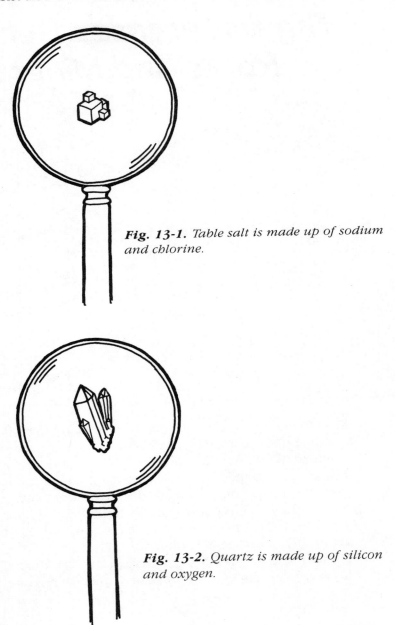

Fig. 13-1. *Table salt is made up of sodium and chlorine.*

Fig. 13-2. *Quartz is made up of silicon and oxygen.*

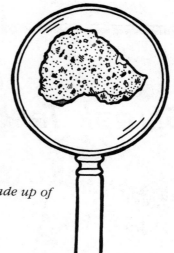

Fig. 13-3. *Granite usually is made up of feldspar, quartz, and mica.*

14
Streak Test of a Mineral

Materials

piece of quartz
piece of ceramic tile

To test the streak of the quartz, carefully scratch a mark across the back, (the dull, unglazed side), of the ceramic tile with the quartz. The streak will be white. The streak of a mineral is the color of its fine powder. It often is obtained by pulverizing the mineral on a piece of unglazed porcelain or by scratching the mineral with a knife or file. The streak of the quartz was white, but often the color of the streak will be very different from the color of the un-powdered mineral.

For example, the mineral hematite is black but has a red streak. The streak of a particular mineral is almost always the same color even though the body color of the mineral varies. For example, the transparent, crystalline mineral fluorite is found in many colors; yellow, green, violet, blue, brown, black, and colorless, but all will have a white streak.

Fig. 14-1. *To streak test, scratch a mark across the back of a piece of ceramic tile.*

15
How to Grow Crystals

Materials

10-12 ounces of white alum
(from grocery store)

1 pint of water

stove

pot

bowl

spoon

cup

Pour the pint of water into the pot and then add about 5 ounces of alum. Have an adult help you heat the water on the stove but don't allow it to boil. Stir the water until the alum dissolves. Continue to add more alum, a little at a time, and stir until no more alum will dissolve. You then will have what is called a saturated solution. Carefully remove the pot from the stove and pour half of the solution into the bowl. Use pot holders or protective gloves. Hot solution can burn!

Set the bowl aside for a few days. Pour the rest of the solution into the jar, leaving any settled material in the pot. Cover the jar with the card to keep out dust particles. After a few days, small crystals will appear in the bowl. Leave them until they are about

Fig. 15-1. *Pour about a pint of water into a pot.*

Fig. 15-2. *Add about five ounces of alum.*

Fig. 15-3. *Heat the water but don't let it boil. Add more alum.*

Fig. 15-4. *Pour some of the solution into a bowl and set it aside.*

Fig. 15-5. *Pour the rest of the solution into a jar, leaving settled material in the pot.*

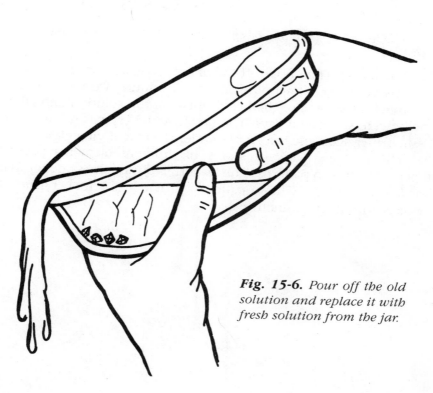

Fig. 15-6. *Pour off the old solution and replace it with fresh solution from the jar.*

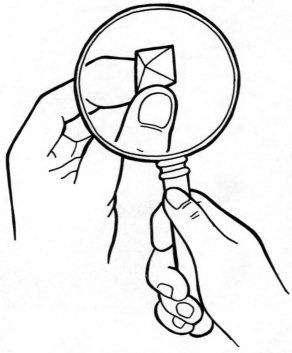

Fig. 15-7. Examine the crystals with a magnifying glass.

1/8 inch across. Then pour off the old solution and dry the crystals with tissue paper. Now pour some fresh solution from the jar into the bowl. Place one of the best crystals in the solution and allow the bowl to set several days. Then remove the crystal and dry it on tissue paper. Examine the crystal under the magnifying glass.

Minerals are made of atoms of different elements packed together in certain patterns. This pattern is always the same for that particular mineral. These patterns provide different types of crystals with their distinctive shape.

16
Testing Chalk with an Acid

Materials

piece of school chalk
medicine dropper
vinegar
knife or single-edged
    safety razor blade
plate

Have an adult help you scrape some chalk powder into a small mound and drop a few drops of vinegar on it. Always be very careful with sharp objects!

You will notice that the chalk powder does not bubble. School chalk is made mostly of gypsum. Strong acids will react with gypsum, but weak acids, like vinegar, cause little or no reaction.

Fig. 16-1. *Scrape some chalk powder into a mound.*

Fig. 16-2. *Add a few drops of vinegar.*

17

Hardness Test For Chalk

Materials

piece of school chalk

your fingernail

Try to make a scratch or groove in the chalk with your fingernail. You should be able to do this easily.

Minerals often are classified by their hardness in numbers from 1 to 10, with 10 being the hardest. A diamond is the hardest mineral, classified with a number 10. Your fingernail has a hardness of about 2.5; it should be harder than the chalk, which has a hardness of 2. A mineral will make a scratch or mark on anything that is of the same hardness, or less hardness, than itself.

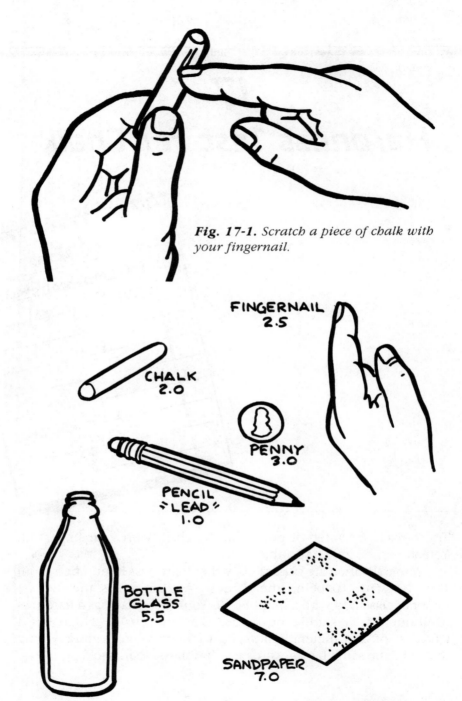

Fig. 17-1. Scratch a piece of chalk with your fingernail.

FINGERNAIL
2.5

CHALK
2.0

PENNY
3.0

PENCIL
LEAD
1.0

BOTTLE
GLASS
5.5

SANDPAPER
7.0

Fig. 17-2. Minerals are classified by their hardness in numbers from one to ten.

18
How to Make Gypsum

Materials

1 cup of plaster of paris
1/2 cup of water
spoon
bowl for mixing
small bowl
2 tablespoons of
cooking oil or grease

Pour 1 cup of plaster of paris into the mixing bowl and add 1/2 cup of water. Stir the mixture until it becomes a smooth, thick paste. Wipe the inside of the small bowl with a thin film of oil to keep the plaster from sticking. Now pour the mixture into the bowl and wait until it hardens. This procedure might take about 30 minutes.

When you heat gypsum, it loses three-fourths of its water. This process is called *calcination*. It changes the gypsum into the fine, white powder called plaster of paris. When you add water to the powder, it turns back into gypsum.

Fig. 18-1. *Pour plaster of paris into a mixing bowl.*

Fig. 18-2. *Add about half as much water.*

Fig. 18-3. *Stir the mixture until it becomes smooth.*

Fig. 18-4. *Apply a thin film of oil to the other bowl to prevent sticking.*

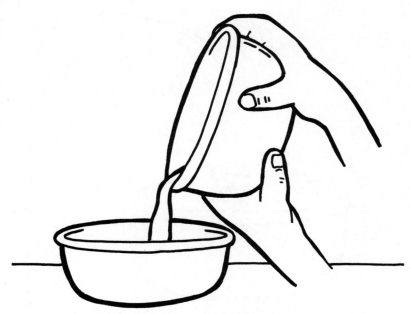

Fig. 18-5. *Pour the mixture into the oiled bowl.*

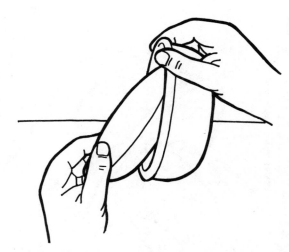

Fig. 18-6. *The mixture will harden and turn into gypsum.*

Gypsum is a white or yellowish-white mineral used to make plaster of paris. When water evaporates from solutions of the mineral, large deposits of gypsum are formed. It is mined to make various products including plaster, cement, and paints.

19
Hardness Test for Gypsum

Materials

piece of gypsum
your fingernail

Try to make a scratch in the gypsum with your fingernail. You should be able to do this, because gypsum has a hardness of 2.

Gypsum might form transparent, colorless crystals called *selenite*, or it might be in a fine, white fibrous mass with a satiny luster called *satin spar*. Alabaster is another variety of gypsum that often is used for statuary and other carvings. Another form of gypsum is called rock gypsum. It is similar to alabaster except that it has a dull luster and usually contains noticeable impurities. It is used in the production of plaster of paris. School chalk is made up of mostly gypsum.

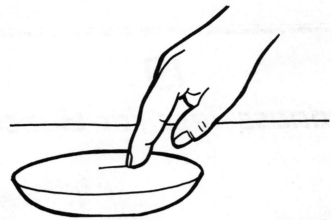

Fig. 19-1. *You should be able to scratch gypsum with your fingernail.*

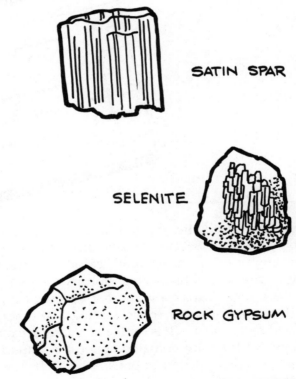

SATIN SPAR

SELENITE

ROCK GYPSUM

Fig. 19-2. *Gypsum can be found in different forms.*

20
Looking at Sand

Materials

magnifying glass
small amount of sand
piece of paper

Spread several grains of sand on the paper. Examine the grains under the magnifying glass. Most of the grains will be parts of solid rocks that have crumbled away. Rocks break apart and crumble from freezing or from the action of wind and rain. Strong waves crashing on a beach wear away the rocks. They also carry pebbles and sand that chip away at the rocks.

Geologists have found many types of minerals in sand. The most common one is quartz. It easily can be recognized because it looks like tiny pieces of broken glass. It is the hardest of all common materials. Only rare minerals such as diamonds, topaz, and corundum are harder. Manufacturers use quartz sand to make chemicals and glass. They also glue loose sand to heavy paper to make sandpaper. Sand also is used in mortar and concrete. Sand used by builders is made up of mostly quartz crystals.

Fig. 20-1. *Spread some sand on a piece of paper.*

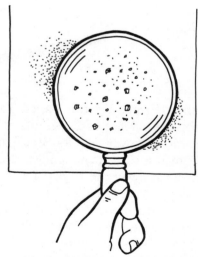

Fig. 20-2. *The most common mineral found in sand is quartz.*

21

Hardness Test for Sandstone

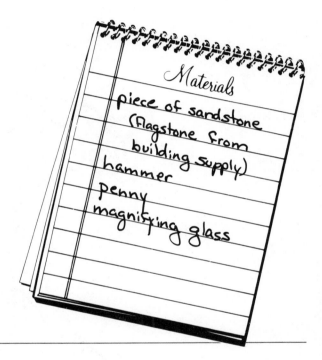

Materials

piece of sandstone
(flagstone from
building supply)
hammer
penny
magnifying glass

Have an adult help you break off a small piece of sandstone with the hammer. Be careful not to get the hammer too close to your fingers.

You will see tiny grains of sand near the break. Examine the grains with the magnifying glass. They should be grains of quartz sand. Some sandstone is very strong while other sandstone is weak and crumbly. It depends on what holds the sandstone together.

If the material called silica holds the sandstone together, the sandstone will be very hard. *Silica* is the name given to silicon dioxide. It is a very common material, widely distributed, and makes up about 60 percent of the earth's crust. If lime holds the

Fig. 21-1. *Break off a piece of sandstone.*

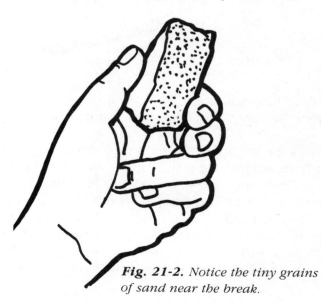

Fig. 21-2. *Notice the tiny grains of sand near the break.*

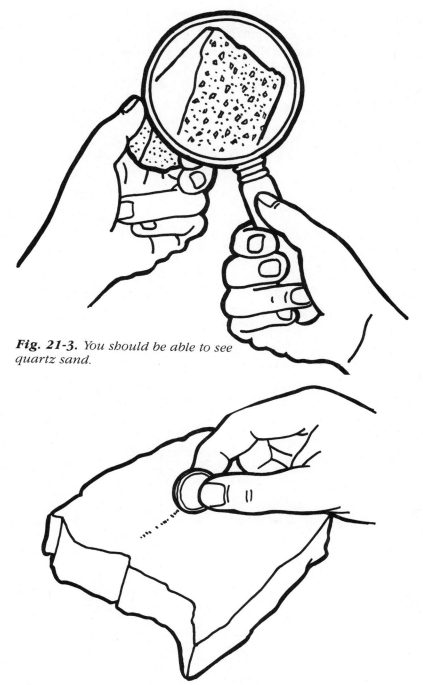

Fig. 21-3. *You should be able to see quartz sand.*

Fig. 21-4. *A penny has a hardness of three. Quartz sand has a hardness of seven.*

sandstone together, the sandstone will be weak and will crumble back into sand between your fingers.

Make a mark across the sandstone with the penny. A copper penny has a hardness of 3. The mark will be along the part that holds the sandstone together because the grains of quartz sand have a hardness of 7.

22
Testing Sandstone with Water and Acid

Materials

2 small pieces of
sandstone
2 glasses
½ cup of water
½ cup of vinegar

Pour some water in one of the glasses and pour vinegar into the other glass. Now drop one of the pieces of sandstone into the glass of water. Bubbles will start rising from the sandstone. Sandstone is porous. Underground deposits of sandstone can hold large amounts of water.

Now drop the other piece of sandstone into the glass of vinegar. Bubbles also will begin to rise from the sandstone. This time, however, there might be more bubbles in the vinegar than in the water. These bubbles mean that the sandstone was held together by lime. When the acid in the vinegar came in contact with the lime, it made carbon dioxide gas. The gas made the extra bubbles.

Fig. 22-1. *Pour water in one glass and vinegar in the other.*

Fig. 22-2. *Drop a piece of sandstone into the water. Notice the amount of bubbles.*

Fig. 22-3. *Drop a piece of sandstone into the vinegar. Lime will cause more bubbles to appear.*

23
How to Make Concrete

Materials

Portland cement
(from hardware store)
water
tablespoon
coffee can

Put about 6 tablespoons of portland cement into the coffee can, and then use the spoon to stir and slowly add water to the powder. Stir the mixture until you have a thick paste.

Now roll the paste into the shape of a natural rock and set it aside until it dries. Drying might take a day. After it dries, it will be concrete. We can think of concrete as man-made rock. Now you can perform scratch tests on your rock for hardness.

Always dispose of any cement mixtures in the trash and never in sinks. Use water to clean the spoon and can.

Fig. 23-1. *Put about six tablespoons of portland cement into a coffee can.*

Fig. 23-2. *Add a little water and stir the mixture into a thick paste.*

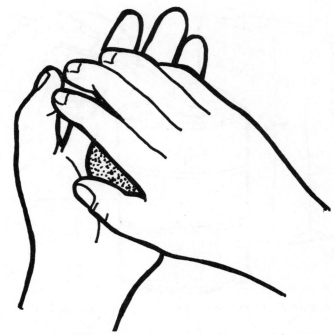

Fig. 23-3. *Roll the paste into the shape of a rock. Set it aside to harden.*

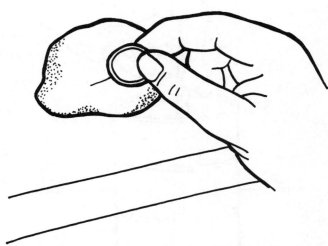

Fig. 23-4. *Scratch test the rock for hardness.*

Fig. 23-5. *Never dispose of cement mixtures in sinks. They will clog drains.*

24
Acid Test for Carbonates

Materials

egg shell
2 tablespoons of
    baking soda
vinegar
small jar
saucer

Pour the baking soda in a small mound in the middle of the saucer, and add a few drops of vinegar. The mixture instantly will start to fizz and bubble. When the acid in the vinegar comes in contact with the carbonates in the baking soda, it produces carbon dioxide gas. Baking soda is a manmade carbonate.

Wash two or three larger pieces of broken egg shell and carefully remove the thin skin attached to the inside of the shell. Now pour about 1/4 cup vinegar into the jar and drop in the pieces of egg shell. The pieces will settle to the bottom, and then you will see bubbles begin to appear and rise to the surface. Enough bubbles will form on the pieces that they might float to the surface. These bubbles are bubbles of carbon dioxide gas.

Carbonates are made by combining carbonic acid, often found in the soil, with a chemical base that contains a metallic element such as calcium or sodium. These two metals form the salts called calcium carbonate and sodium carbonate. Calcium carbonate is found in limestone, marble, and chalk. It is also the main material in egg shells, oyster shells, pearls, and coral. Carbonates fizz or bubble, giving off carbon dioxide gas, when they come in contact with acid.

Fig. 24-1. *Pour a mound of baking soda on a saucer.*

Fig. 24-2. *Add a few drops of vinegar to the baking soda.*

Fig. 24-3. *Bubbles quickly form from carbon dioxide gas.*

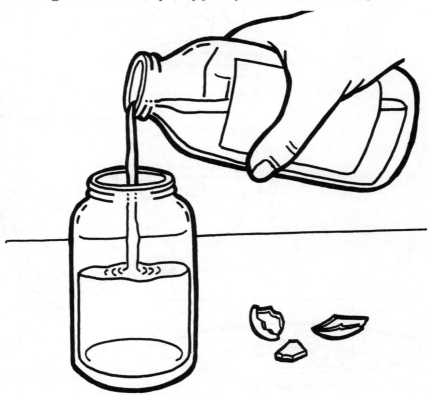

Fig. 24-4. *Pour vinegar into a jar.*

Fig. 24-5. Drop pieces of egg shell into the vinegar. Notice bubbles appear.

25
Scratch Testing Limestone

Materials

piece of limestone

Knife

hammer

Have an adult help you break off a piece of limestone with the hammer. It will break forming jagged edges. You cannot break limestone into layers or split it, but you can carve it easily and cut it in any way without splitting it.

Very carefully, try to make a scratch across the limestone with the knife. Limestone has a hardness of about 3, but other minerals in it might make it a little harder. The knife blade should have a hardness of a little over 5. So you can scratch ordinary limestone with a knife.

Limestone is a rock made up mostly of calcium carbonate. It is usually a grayish color, but all colors of limestone from white to black have been found.

Fig. 25-1. *Break off a piece of limestone.*

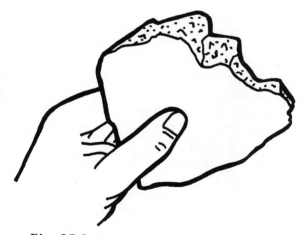

Fig. 25-2. *Notice the edges will be jagged.*

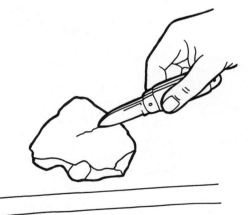

Fig. 25-3. *Limestone can be carved, but not split.*

26
How to Tell Limestone From Quartzite

Quartzite is a type of sandstone. It is metamorphic. This word means that it was formed slowly, and gradually changed from sand to stone. Like the original sand, it is made mostly of quartz. When split, it does not cleave along parallel lines like most metamorphic rocks. Limestone usually forms when calcium carbonates are dissolved in the waters of shallow seas. Sometimes it is hard to tell limestone from quartzite.

Very carefully, try scratching each rock with the knife. The limestone can be scratched, but not quartzite. Limestone has a hardness of about 3 or 4.

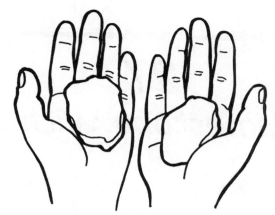

Fig. 26-1. *Compare a piece of quartzite to a piece of limestone.*

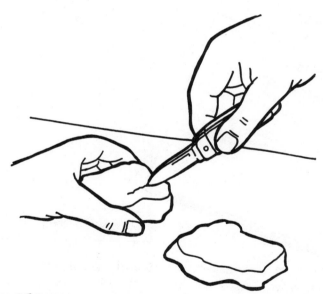

Fig. 26-2. *Limestone has a hardness of about three or four.*

27

Testing Limestone With an Acid

Materials

piece of limestone
medicine dropper
steel file
1 tablespoon of vinegar

Scrape the piece of limestone with the file to collect a small mound of powder. Now drop a few drops of vinegar on the powder. It should bubble. Limestone is formed when the remains of tiny sea animals sink to the sea floor and, over thousands of years, build up layers that turn into the limestone we use today. It is made up mostly of calcium carbonate. Calcium carbonate causes the limestone to bubble if it comes in contact with an acid.

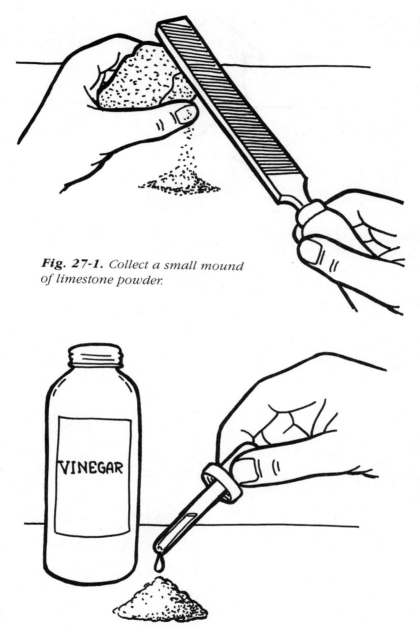

Fig. 27-1. *Collect a small mound of limestone powder.*

Fig. 27-2. *Add a few drops of vinegar.*

Fig. 27-3. Limestone will bubble if it comes in contact with an acid.

28
Hardness Test for Graphite

Materials
pencil lead (No. 2 pencil)
your fingernail

Try scratching the pencil lead with your fingernail. It easily will leave a groove in the lead. Your fingernail has a hardness of 2.5 while the pencil lead, made from graphite, is softer.

Graphite is one of the softest minerals. It has a hardness of 1. Graphite is mixed with clay and then baked at a high temperature to make lead for pencils. The hardness of the lead depends on the proportion of clay to graphite. A No. 2 pencil lead contains about two-thirds graphite and one-third clay.

Graphite was used first in pencils in 1550. Artificial graphite has been made since 1896. Manufactured graphite can be substituted now for nearly all the uses of natural graphite. It not only is used in making pencils, but its softness and greasiness makes it useful in manufacturing paints and lubricants. This soft, greasy, black material is the same chemical substance as the hardest known mineral, the diamond.

Carbon atoms in diamonds are locked together in three directions. This bond makes diamonds very hard. The carbon atoms in graphite are joined in only two directions, forming thin plates that easily slide over each other. This structure causes graphite to be slippery.

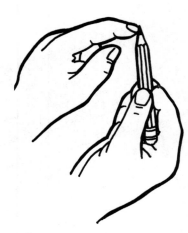

Fig. 28-1. *Your fingernail is harder than graphite.*

29
Hardness Test for Metals

Carefully try scratching the nail with the penny. Now try scratching the penny with the nail. The nail should mark the penny. The copper penny has a hardness of 3, while the nail has a hardness of about 4.

Now try to scratch the steel file with the nail. Then try scratching the nail with the file. The file should scratch the nail. The steel file has a hardness of about 6.5.

Fig. 29-1. *Try to scratch a nail with a penny.*

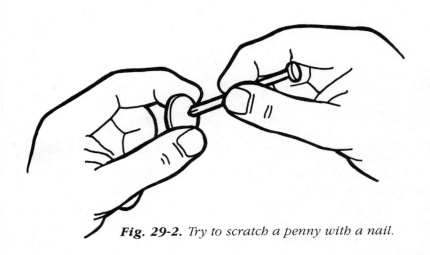

Fig. 29-2. *Try to scratch a penny with a nail.*

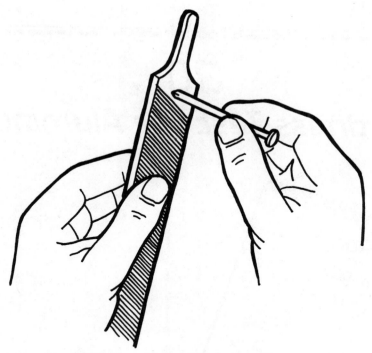

Fig. 29-3. *Try to scratch a steel file with a nail.*

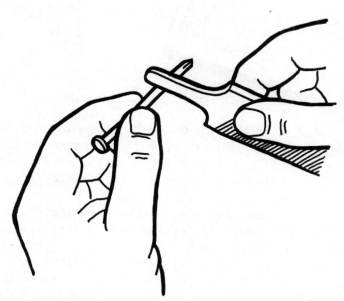

Fig. 29-4. *Try to scratch a nail with the steel file.*

30
Hardness Test for Aluminum

Materials

copper penny
aluminum pan

Try scratching the aluminum pan with the penny. The copper penny will scratch the aluminum pan. The copper penny has a hardness of 3. Aluminum is a soft metal with a hardness of about 2. Manganese is added to the aluminum used to make cooking utensils so it will be a little harder.

Aluminum is one of the most common metals, but it never occurs as a metal in nature like copper or gold. It is found only in compounds with other metals.

Aluminum compounds make up more than 15 percent of the earth's crust. The oxide and other compounds of aluminum found in soils, rocks, and minerals are hard to break down to the metal.

Aluminum can be made inexpensively only from an ore called *bauxite*. Bauxite is normally found in hard, rocklike formations, but it also can be as soft as mud.

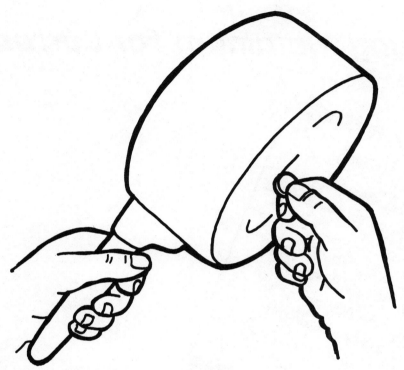

Fig. 30-1. *Scratch test an aluminum pot with a penny.*

31
Testing Aluminum for Corrosion

Materials

3 small glasses
3 strips of aluminum foil
¼ cup water
¼ cup vinegar
3 tablespoons salt
1 teaspoon baking soda

Smooth out each strip of aluminum foil with your finger. Lower a part of one end into each glass and bend the other end over the rim to hold it in place. Allow an inch or two of the strip to lay against the bottom of the glass.

Now pour some vinegar in the first glass so that it covers the bottom part of the strip of aluminum. Then mix a strong solution of salt and water and pour it in the second glass. Dissolve 1 teaspoon of baking soda in a small amount of water and pour it in the third glass. Set the glasses aside for several days.

Examine each strip of aluminum and compare the part that was submerged in liquid and the part that was exposed to just air. You might notice that a weak acid, like vinegar, dulled the surface a little. Most strong acids will act on aluminum. Salt tends to corrode the surface of aluminum along with alkalis like bicarbonate of soda or baking soda. Aluminum is strong and light. Because it is not affected by water, it doesn't rust. Aluminum has a thin oxide coating. This natural coating provides protection for the surface of the aluminum.

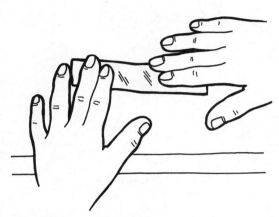

Fig. 31-1. *Smooth the strips of aluminum with your finger.*

Fig. 31-2. *Place the ends of each strip into separate glasses.*

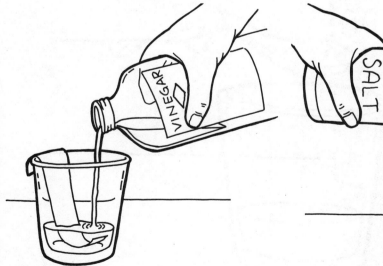

Fig. 31-3. *Cover the bottom of the first strip with vinegar.*

Fig. 31-4. *Mix a strong solution of salt and water.*

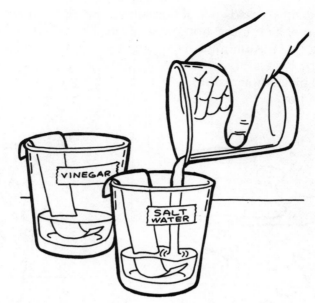

Fig. 31-5. *Cover the bottom of the second strip with salt water.*

Fig. 31-6. *Mix a solution of baking soda and water.*

Fig. 31-7. *Cover the bottom of the third strip with the baking soda solution.*

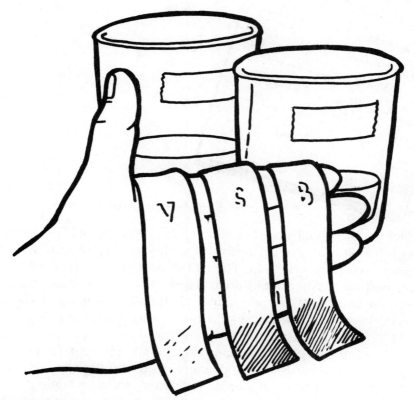

Fig. 31-8. *Examine the strips after several days. Alkalis will corrode aluminum.*

32
Chemical Weathering of Rocks

Materials

nail
medicine dropper
saucer
spoon
glass
vinegar
water

Place about two tablespoons of water in the saucer and stir in a few drops of vinegar. Place a clean nail in the saucer and turn the glass upside down over the nail. The nail should be covered partly with the mixture of vinegar and water. The glass is used to hold moist air over the nail. Set the experiment aside for a few hours until the nail begins to rust. Iron will rust in ordinary water and moist air, but the acid in the vinegar speeds up the rusting.

By combining with, or removing, certain elements in minerals, water and air change the appearance and composition of rocks. One process is called *oxidation*. Oxidation occurs when oxygen is added to the minerals of rocks, especially to the iron compounds, to form oxides. When the nail rusts, it first becomes dull, then rusty, and eventually will turn to a powder or iron rust. Moisture and oxygen acting upon the minerals that contain iron produce an iron rust like that from the rusting nail. The red, brown, and yellow colors so often found in rocks and soils are stains from the rusting or decay of iron-bearing minerals.

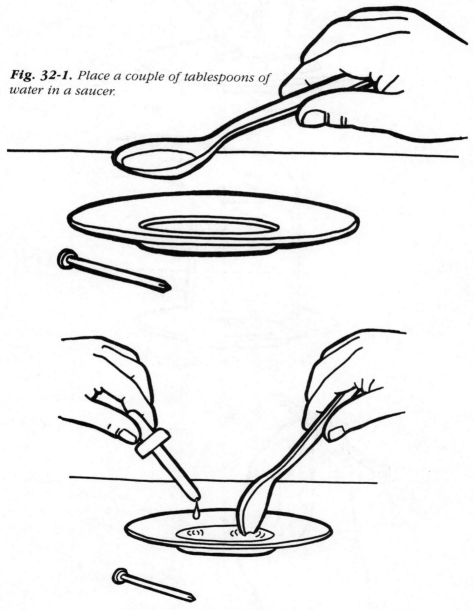

Fig. 32-1. *Place a couple of tablespoons of water in a saucer.*

Fig. 32-2. *Add a few drops of vinegar.*

Fig. 32-3. *Place a nail in the saucer.*

Fig. 32-4. *Cover the nail with a glass.*

Fig. 32-5. *Acid in the vinegar speeds rusting.*

33

Hardness Test of Metals and Glass

Try scratching the glass with the steel file. The file should scratch the glass. The glass has a hardness of about 5.5 and the file has a hardness of 6.5. Now try to scratch the smooth part of the steel file with the sandpaper. The sandpaper should scratch the file because the sandpaper has a hardness of about 7.

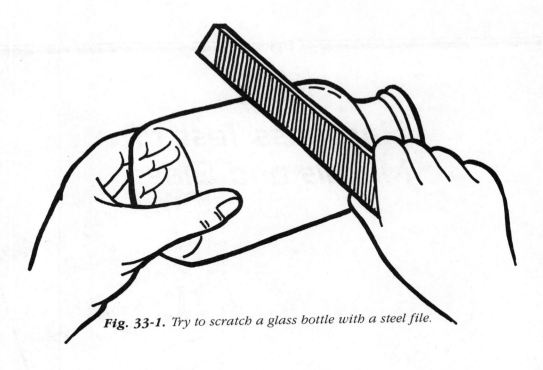

Fig. 33-1. *Try to scratch a glass bottle with a steel file.*

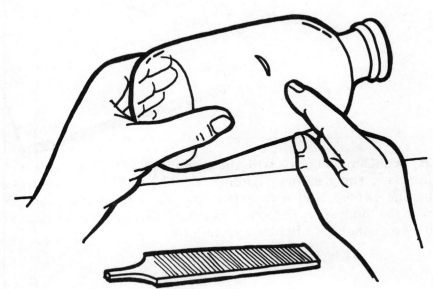

Fig. 33-2. *The file should scratch the glass.*

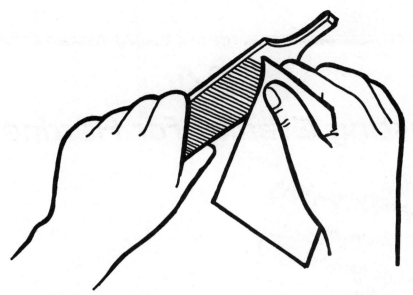

Fig. 33-3. *Try to scratch the steel file with sandpaper.*

Fig. 33-4. *The sandpaper should scratch the file.*

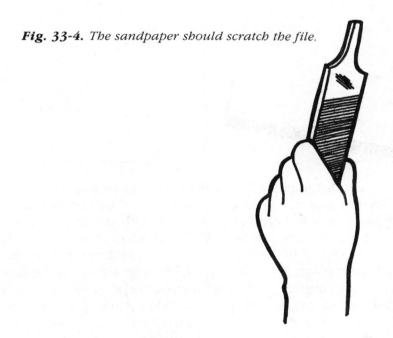

34
Testing Granite for Hardness

Materials

piece of granite
steel file
emery paper
magnifying glass

Try to scratch the granite with the file. It should scratch some parts easily. Try to polish the granite with the emery paper. Moisten the granite and you will be able to polish it with the emery paper. Emery paper has a hardness of 9. *Granite* is a hard crystalline rock, made up mostly of mineral crystals such as feldspar and quartz. Granite is light colored, and its crystals are large enough to be seen without a magnifying glass. The feldspar crystals are generally rectangular in shape, and are colored a dull white, gray, or pink. Feldspar has a hardness of 6. The quartz will be clear, much like glass. Dark-colored minerals, mostly hornblende and black mica, are scattered in the mass of quartz and feldspar crystals. The individual crystals making up most granite are from a fraction of an inch to about a half inch wide. Coarse-grained granite contains crystals of feldspar from one to several inches long.

Fig. 34-1. *Try to scratch a piece of granite with a steel file.*

Fig. 34-2. *Try to scratch a piece of granite with emery paper.*

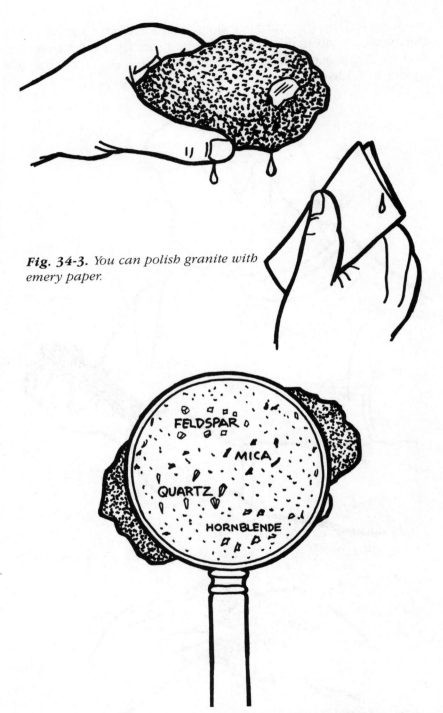

Fig. 34-3. *You can polish granite with emery paper.*

Fig. 34-4. *Examine a piece of granite with a magnifying glass.*

35

Testing Granite with an Acid

Materials

piece of granite
medicine dropper
steel file
½ teaspoon vinegar

Use the file to scratch some powdered granite into a small mound. Now slowly drop the vinegar, drop by drop, on top of the mound of powder. It should not bubble. It is made up chiefly of quartz and feldspar. *Feldspars* are the most common rock-forming minerals.

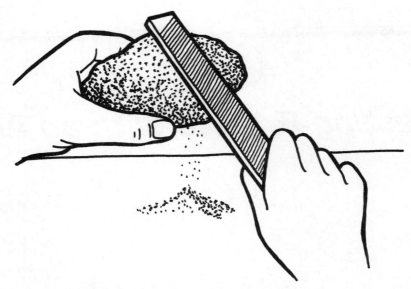

Fig. 35-1. *Collect a small mound of granite powder.*

Fig. 35-2. *Add a few drops of vinegar to see if it bubbles.*

36
Testing Marble for Hardness

Materials

piece of marble
copper penny
nail
steel file

Carefully try scratching the marble first with the penny, then with the nail, and then with the file. The marble has a hardness of 3 and might or might not be scratched by the penny because the penny also has a hardness of about 3. The nail should scratch the marble because it has a hardness of about 4. The file easily should scratch the marble because it has a hardness of about 6.5.

All marble is made up of the minerals calcite or dolomite, which if pure, is perfectly white. Colored marble is caused by the presence of other minerals or staining material that is mixed with the calcite or dolomite. Red, brown, and yellow tones are caused by oxides of iron. Green shades might be caused by chlorite or serpentine. Chlorite is a salt of aluminum, magnesium, and iron with water. Serpentine is a mineral or rock made up of hydrated salt of magnesium. Carbonate materials altered to graphite makes marble gray or black.

Marble is limestone that has been changed through the action of heat and pressure far below the earth's surface.

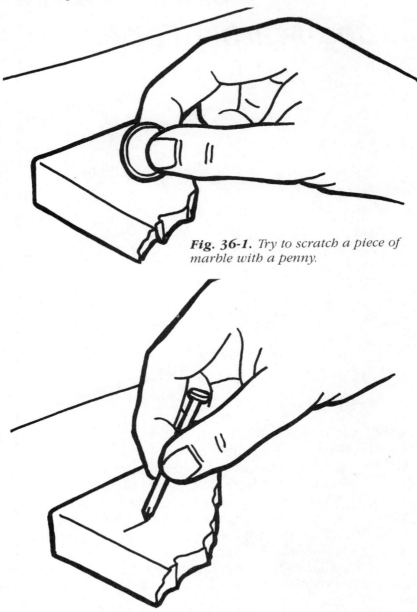

Fig. 36-1. *Try to scratch a piece of marble with a penny.*

Fig. 36-2. *Try to scratch a piece of marble with a nail.*

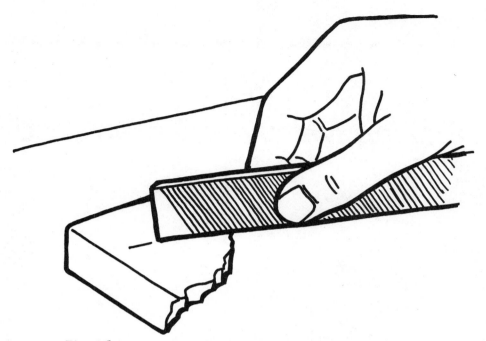

Fig. 36-3. *A steel file easily should scratch a piece of marble.*

37
Testing Marble with an Acid

Materials

piece of marble
steel file
½ tablespoon vinegar
medicine dropper

Use the file to collect a small amount of marble powder. Then drop a few drops of vinegar on the powder. It could bubble. Marble is made up mostly of calcite or dolomite. Calcite is a form of calcium carbonate. It easily reacts with a cold acid. Dolomite is a mineral made up of carbonates of calcium and magnesium. It is often very like calcite except that it is harder and does not readily react with a cold acid.

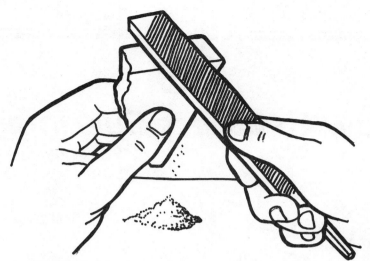

Fig. 37-1. *Collect a small mound of marble powder.*

Fig. 37-2. *Add a few drops of vinegar to see if it bubbles.*

38
How to Collect Specimens

Materials

geologist's hammer
gloves
goggles
folding magnifying lens
(magnification of 8 or 10)
felt pen
notebook
paper towels or
newspaper

Wear boots and sturdy clothes because you probably will get dirty doing field work. Some field work can be done alone, while other field work should be done with a friend. In both cases, *always* tell someone exactly where you are going and when you should be back. Don't take any risks. For example, working at the base of a cliff might bring down an avalanche of rocks, so always be very careful.

Wear safety goggles to protect your eyes from flying chips of rocks. Break off pieces of rock with your hammer, then examine them with the magnifying glass. Number it with the felt pen and describe the specimen in the notebook and note where you found it.

Fig. 38-1. *Wear sturdy clothes and try to go collecting with a friend.*

Fig. 38-2. *Wear safety goggle when chipping rocks.*

You can wrap the specimen in a paper towel or newspaper, to protect it from other samples. You can use a strong back-pack to carry the rocks back home.

Fig. 38-3. *Examine pieces of rock with a magnifying glass.*

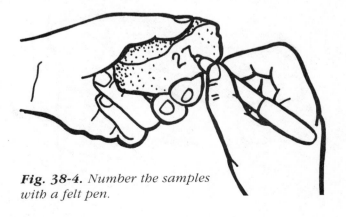

Fig. 38-4. *Number the samples with a felt pen.*

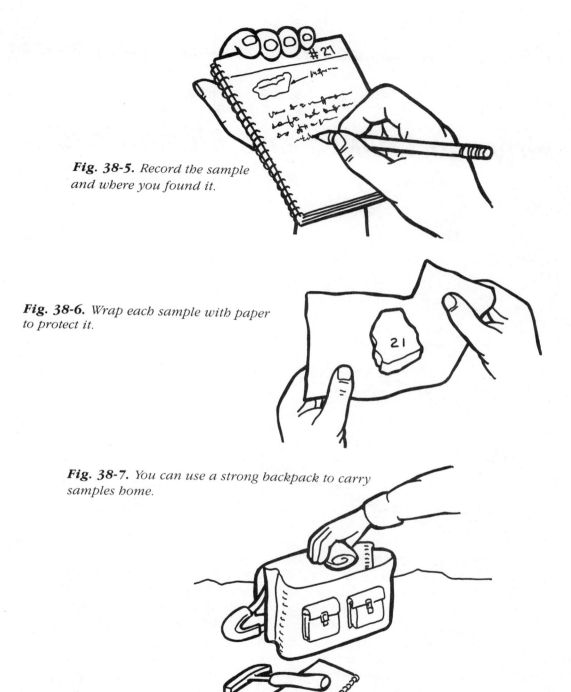

Fig. 38-5. *Record the sample and where you found it.*

Fig. 38-6. *Wrap each sample with paper to protect it.*

Fig. 38-7. *You can use a strong backpack to carry samples home.*

39
How to Collect and Clean Fossils

Materials

geologist's hammer
goggles
small screwdriver
small cold-chisel
old toothbrush or
paint brush
paper towel or
newspaper
magnifying glass

You will find almost all fossils in rocks that have been built up in layers from small particles. These rocks are called *sedimentary rocks*. These sedimentary rocks lie beneath about three-fourths of the surface of the land area of the earth. Fossils might be found anywhere that the sedimentary rock is exposed, but the best places to find fossils are areas where the wind and water have cut deep into the rocks and exposed large areas. In these places, the fossils are closer to the surface, or they might even be exposed.

When you find a fossil, study the rock it's in. Carefully tap the rock so that it will break along its natural lines of weakness and leave the fossil intact. You can use the screwdriver or chisel to pry or break the rock free. Wrap the rock in a paper towel and take it home to trim. There, place it in a box of sand or on an old pillow or hold it with wooden clamps so the rock won't move about while you work. A magnifying glass mounted on an arm will be a big help. Use the small tools to do the cleaning and trimming, then use the brush to do the final cleaning.

Again, before you go out fossil-hunting either take a buddy or an adult with you, or at least tell someone where exactly you are going and when you should be back.

Fig. 39-1. *Fossils usually are found in rocks formed into layers.*

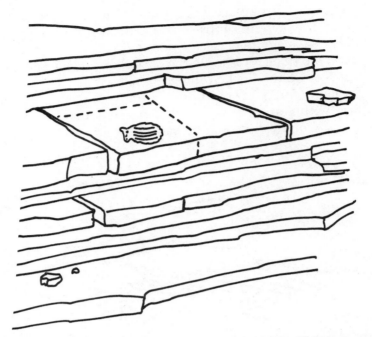

Fig. 39-2. *Try to break the rock so that the fossil will be intact.*

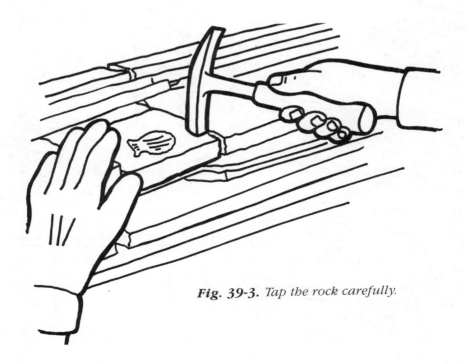

Fig. 39-3. *Tap the rock carefully.*

Fig. 39-4. *Use a screwdriver or chisel to pry the rock free.*

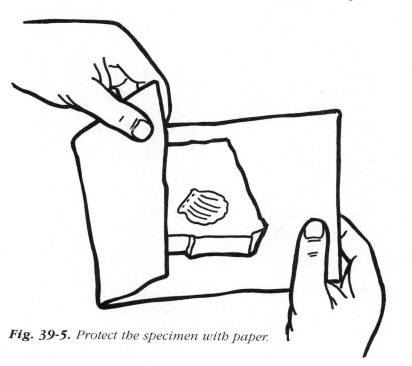

Fig. 39-5. *Protect the specimen with paper.*

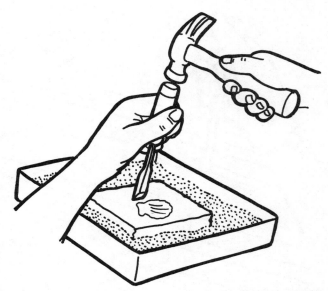

Fig. **39-6.** *Place the specimen in a box of sand so it won't move.*

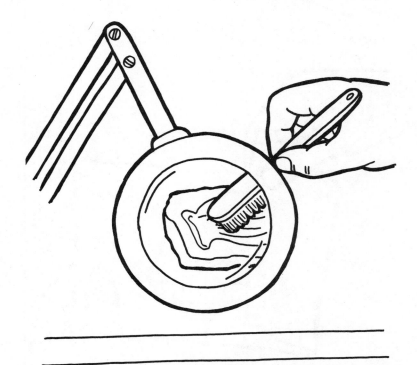

Fig. **39-7.** *You can use an old toothbrush for final cleaning.*

Science Fair Projects

Science fairs are common occurrences and are nothing to cause a panic. A properly planned project can be an exciting experience. The important part is the planning, if you want the project to be successful. You might want to start by dividing your science fair project into a series of easy steps. For example:

1. Choosing the topic.
2. Questions and hypothesis. The hypothesis is just your opinion of what the results of the experiment will be.
3. Doing the experiment.
4. The results of the experiment and your conclusions.

One of the most important parts of the planning stage is selecting the topic. This selection requires some research and a lot of thought (Fig. 40-1). If you select a topic too quickly, you might find later that the materials were too expensive or not even available or that the project was just too complicated to complete. If this happens, you might abandon the project and it might be too late to start another.

It is important to research your subject. This research can include writing a research paper (Fig. 40-2). This paper will help you gather important information and narrow down your subject to a specific topic. You probably want to write a report on your experiment. The report will explain what you wanted to prove or what question you wanted to answer. You might want to use graphs or charts to help explain your experiment. The report should describe your experiment, the results of your experiment, and the conclusions you made based on the results of the experiment.

Fig. 40-1. *Science fair projects require planning and research.*

Fig. 40-2. *You might want to write a report.*

When choosing a project, select a topic that you are really interested in or one that you want to learn more about. Try to chose something that you can become enthused about. Don't make your experiment too complicated. You might have problems locating the necessary materials. Materials for experiments often can be found in items that usually are thrown away (Fig. 40-3). These materials include such items as empty coffee cans, plastic or glass bottles, cardboard tubes from paper towels, and wooden spools from sewing thread. You might want to build a model for your display. You often can make these from cardboard or wood.

Fig. 40-3. You often can use throwaway items.

After you have selected a topic for your project, narrow it down to a specific question you want to answer or a particular point you want to prove. Don't generalize. Pick a specific problem to solve. For example, if you are interested in the different kinds of surfaces of the earth, you could use layers of different colored clays on a piece of stretched rubber (Fig. 40-4). When the rubber is released slowly, the layers of clay would push together like the different layers of the earth's crust and it would show how mountains are formed.

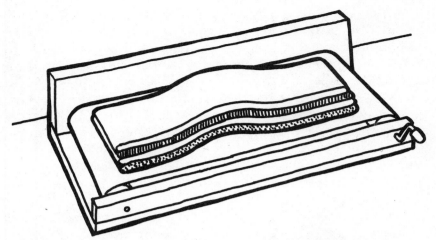

Fig. 40-4. *Use layers of different colored clay to show how mountains were formed.*

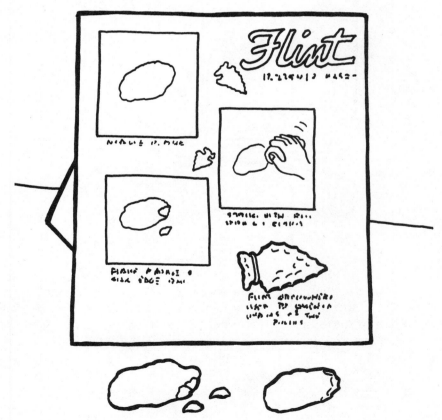

Fig. 40-5. *Early weapons and tools were made from flint.*

In the beginning, your experiment might be very simple, but through research and using your imagination, you can develop and expand most any simple experiment into a very interesting project. It is important for your science fair project to be educational, but it is also important for you to have fun while you discover something new. Geology is an important earth science that is essential to human progress.

If you wanted to show how early civilizations used geology, you could show how some lumps of rocks, called nodules, found in sedimentary rocks, contain flint. The sharpness of its broken edges made flint an ideal material for man's first weapons and tools (Fig. 40-5).

If you are interested in soil and water conservation, you could build a model of a landscape and show how vegetation is used to hold the soil together and protect it from erosion (Fig. 40-6). This vegetation also allows the water more time to soak into the ground.

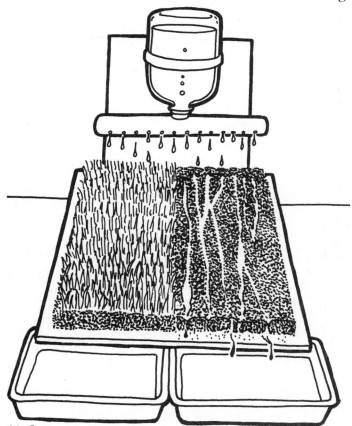

Fig. 40-6. *Vegetation holds the soil together and prevents erosion.*

Most people display their projects on some type of table or platform. You could set your experiment up in front of cardboard or wooden panels. Divide the panels into three sections. (Fig. 40-7). Angle the two end sections forward slightly so that the panel will stand by itself, like the back part of a theater stage. You can use each section of the panel to show information about your experiment (Fig. 40-8). The left section could show the purpose of your experiment. This section should include why you chose the experiment and what you want to prove. The middle section of the panel could be a diagram of your experiment and why it was built the way it was. The right section of the panel could display the results of your experiment and your conclusions. This section might also include any possible uses, or applications, of this information. You should include any way it might help our environment.

Fig. 40-7. *You can display your experiment in front of a panel.*

Fig. 40-8. *You can display information about your experiment on the panel.*

Glossary

alabaster   white, translucent gypsum with a fine texture.

alkalis   any soluble mineral salt, or mixture of salts, found in soil and capable of neutralizing acids.

anticlines   a shapely arched fold of stratified rock, from whose central axis the strata slope downward in opposite directions; opposed to synclines.

atom   any of the smallest particles of an element that combine with similar particles of other elements to produce compounds.

bauxite   the claylike ore, mainly hydrated aluminum oxide, from which aluminum is obtained.

calcination   heat to a high temperature.

calcium   a soft, silver-white, metallic chemical element found in limestone, marble, and chalk.

capillary action   the movement, caused by surface tension and other forces, of a liquid through tiny openings in a solid.

chloride   the compound in which chlorine is combined with another element.

compound   a material made up of two or more elements joined together.

element   a material made up of only one kind of atom.

evaporate   to change a liquid into a vapor.

erosion   the wearing away of the earth, usually by wind or water.

feldspar   any of several crystalline minerals made up of aluminum silicates with sodium, potassium, or calcium usually glassy and moderately hard.

granite   a very hard crystal rock, gray to pink in color, consisting of feldspar, quartz, and smaller amounts of other minerals.

graphite   a soft, black luster form of carbon found in nature.

halite   native sodium chloride; rock salt.

hematite   a brownish red or black iron ore.

hornblende a black rock-forming mineral.

hypothesis a guess used by scientists to explain how or why something happens.

humus brown or black substance formed from the partial decay of plant or animal (organic) matter.

iron a white, malleable, metallic element that can be magnetized easily.

lime a white substance, calcium oxide, obtained by the action of heat on limestone, shales, and other materials containing calcium carbonate.

limestone rock consisting mainly of calcium carbonate often composed of the organic remains of sea animals such as mollusk, coral, etc.

manganese a grayish-white, metallic, chemical element, usually hard and brittle, which rusts like iron but is not magnetic.

marble a hard crystal or granular metamorphic limestone, white and variously colored, and sometimes streaked or modeled.

metamorphic rock that has been changed by pressure, heat, or water to become more compact and crystalline.

mica any of a group of minerals that crystallize in a thin, somewhat flexible, translucent or colored, easily separated layers resistant to heat and electricity.

minerals an inorganic substance occurring naturally in the earth and having a consistent and distinctive set of physical properties.

molecules the smallest particle of an element or compound that can exist in the free state and still retain the characteristics of the element or compound.

nodules a small, usually rounded body, harder than the surrounding material.

oxidation combining with oxygen.

potassium a soft, silver-white, waxlike, metallic, chemical element that oxidizes rapidly when exposed to air.

quartz a brilliant, hexagonally-crystalline mineral, silicon dioxide, occurring in abundance, most often in a colorless, transparent form.

quartzite compact, granular rock composed of quartz.

sandstone a compound sedimentary rock made up largely of sand grains, mainly quartz, held together by silica, lime, etc.

saturated having absorbed all that can be taken up.

sedimentary rock formed of fragments transported, usually by water, from their original place.

selenite   a kind of gypsum occurring in crystals.

silica   a hard, glassy mineral found in a variety of forms such as quartz, sand, and opal.

silicon   a nonmetallic chemical element occurring in several forms, found always in combination, and more abundant in nature than any other element except oxygen.

sodium   a soft, silver-white, alkaline metallic chemical element having a waxlike consistency.

synclines   a down fold in stratified rock, from whose central axis the beds rise upward and outward in opposite directions; opposed to anticlines.

Index

hardness-testing (*con't.*)
  gypsum, 57-58, 61
  limestone, 78-79
  marble, 105-107
  quartzite, 78-79
  sandstone, 61-64
  steel, 85-87, 97-99
  water, 26-29
humus, 12, 18-19
Hutton, James, viii
hydrologic (water) cycle, 25
hypotheses, 119, 121

I _____

ice, rock fractures and breakage,
  8-11

L _____

limestone, 20-22
  acid-testing, 65-67, 80-82
  hardness testing, 78-79
  marble, 105-107
  quartzite vs., hardness testing,
    78-79
  scratch-testing, 76-77
Lyell, Charles, viii

M _____

marble, 20-22
  acid-testing, 108-109
  hardness-testing, 105-107
metals
  aluminum, hardness-testing,
    88-89
  copper, hardness-testing, 85-
    87
  corrosion, oxidation, rust, 90-
    96
  steel, hardness testing, 85-87,
    97-99
metamorphic rocks, 78-79
mineral-testing water, 23-25
minerals
  chalk, 51-52
  granite, 100-102
  graphite, 83-84
  gypsum, 57-58, 61
  limestone, 78-79
  marble, 105-107
  quartzite, 78-79
  rocks vs. minerals, 39-41
  sandstone, 61-64

scratch-testing, limestone, 76-
  77
streak testing, 42-43
minerology, viii

O _____

ocean's salt, 30-32
oil, viii
overfolds, 4-7
oxidation, 94-96
  aluminum, 90-93

P _____

plant roots breaking up rocks,
  14-17
plaster of paris, 53-56
plate tectonics, vii

Q _____

quartz, 39-40, 59-60, 61-64,
  100-102
  hardness testing, 78-79
  limestone vs., hardness test-
    ing, 78-79

R _____

report writing, 119, 120
research, 119, 120
rocks
  chemical-weathering, 94-96
  folding and squeezing, 4-7
  fractures and breakage, 8-11
  minerals vs. rocks, 39-41
  plant action on rocks, 14-17
  sedimentation, 18-19
rust, 94-96

S _____

salt
  crystal structure, 33-38
  ocean water, 30-32
  water-absorption, 33-34
sand, 12, 59-60
sandstone
  acid-testing, 65-67
  hardness testing, 61-64
science fair projects, 119-125
  display panels, 124-125
  experiments, 119-123
  questions and hypothesis,
    119, 121
  report writing, 119, 120

132 *Index*

research, 119, 120
  topic selection, 119, 121
scratch-testing limestone, 76-77
sedimentation, 18-19
silica, 61-64
silts, 18-19
sodium carbonate, 29, 73-75
soft water, 26-29
soil
  sedimentation in water, 18-19
  soil analysis, 12-13
specimen collection, 110-113
steel, hardness testing, 85-87,
  97-99
streak test for minerals, 42-43
subsoils, 12
symbols used in this book, ix-x

synclines, 4-7

T _____
topsoils, 12

V _____
volcanoes, vii

W _____
water
  hardness-testing, 26-29
  hydrologic cycle, 25
  ice heaving, 8-11
  mineral-testing, 23-25
  ocean's salt, 30-32
  salt absorbs water, 33-34
  sedimentation, 18-19